HISTORIC
COMMUNITIES

In the Barn

Bobbie Kalman

 Crabtree Publishing Company

HISTORIC
COMMUNITIES

Created by Bobbie Kalman

*In loving memory of my grandparents,
whose barn was a magical playland*

Editor-in-Chief
Bobbie Kalman

Research
Teresa Rigg
Lise Gunby

Writing team
Bobbie Kalman
Niki Walker

Managing editor
Lynda Hale

Editors
Niki Walker
Greg Nickles
Petrina Gentile

Computer design
Lynda Hale

Special thanks to
Steve Davis and Living History Farms, Iowa;
John Johnson and Georgia Agrirama; Leigh Adamson,
Brian Adamson, and the Genesee Country Museum;
Black Creek Pioneer Village, Metro Toronto and
Region Conservation Authority; Mandy Bidwell
and Bronte Provincial Park; Priscilla and Karl Baker;
Kathleen Stocking and the New York State
Historical Association

Separations and film
Dot 'n Line Image Inc.

Printer
Worzalla Publishing Company

Crabtree Publishing Company

350 Fifth Avenue
Suite 3308
New York
N.Y. 10118

360 York Road, RR 4
Niagara-on-the-Lake
Ontario, Canada
L0S 1J0

73 Lime Walk
Headington
Oxford OX3 7AD
United Kingdom

Copyright © **1997 CRABTREE PUBLISHING COMPANY**. All
rights reserved. No part of this publication may be reproduced,
stored in a retrieval system or be transmitted in any form or by
any means, electronic, mechanical, photocopying, recording, or
otherwise, without the prior written permission of Crabtree
Publishing Company.

Cataloging in Publication Data
Kalman, Bobbie
  In the Barn

(Historic communities series)
Includes index.
ISBN 0-86505-433-9 (library bound) ISBN 0-86505-463-0 (pbk.)
This book examines the barn as the center of farm life for early
settlers in North America.

1. Farm life - North America - History - Juvenile literature.
2. Barns - North America - History - Juvenile literature.
3. Frontier and pioneer life - North America - Juvenile literature.
I. Title. II. Series: Kalman, Bobbie. Historic communities.

S519.K36 1996   j631.2'2'097   LC 96-44509
                                                          CIP

Contents

Barns of the pioneers

Early pioneers came to North America with dreams of having a large family farm. When they arrived, however, they found only wilderness. To build a farm and grow crops, they had to clear the land of hundreds of trees. With the first few trees they chopped down, family members quickly built a rough log cabin for themselves and a **lean-to** shelter for their few animals. A lean-to has only three walls, one of which is the sloped roof that reaches the ground.

The first barns

The next job was to build a small barn before winter came. This simple barn was made of logs and had a dirt floor. It had a **thatched** roof made with bundles of grass. Thatched roofs leaked, easily caught fire, and did not keep out the wind. The settlers soon replaced these roofs with ones made of sod, bark, or hollowed logs.

*The smaller building in the picture above is a log **shanty**. A shanty is a small, roughly constructed building. These barns were common on pioneer farms.*

Bigger farms, bigger barns

Each year the family cleared more land on their farm. Within a few years they had vast fields of crops as well as many animals. They needed a bigger barn to house their livestock and large harvests. Some farmers built a separate barn for their crops and animals, and others built one barn to shelter both. The barn was the most important building on the farm, and soon it became the largest and most expensive, as well.

The heart of the farm

A barn was not just a building in which to store crops and house animals. It was the center of activity on a pioneer farm. There were many chores to be done in the barn, such as repairing tools, shearing sheep, and husking corn. Families often invited neighbors for a work party and dance inside the barn.

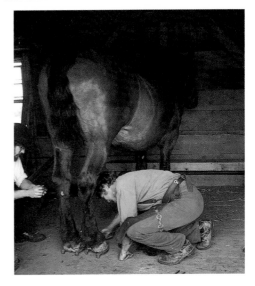

In pioneer times, even tradespeople such as blacksmiths and carpenters farmed. Some also used their barn as a place of business.

The pioneer family on this farm has cleared many acres of land and built a sturdy barn and stable for the crops and livestock.

The barn above is a Dutch barn. It looks similar to an English barn, but its doors are in a different spot. They are beneath the roof's peak, whereas the doors of an English barn are on the side, under the roof's slope.

The lower level of a bank barn housed food bins and a root cellar in addition to livestock. The earth surrounding this level protected foods such as turnips from heat and frost.

Types of barns

Before farmers built a large barn, there were several factors they had to consider. Which building materials were available? What was the weather like in the area? Would the barn shelter crops, livestock, or both? Barns were built in many different styles and sizes to meet the needs of different farmers.

English barn

An English barn had two levels. The bottom floor housed livestock, and the upper one stored straw and hay. Unlike early log barns, which were built by stacking logs one on top of the other, English barns were built by constructing a wooden frame and covering it with wooden planks. To make the frame, a farmer chopped down trees and shaped them into square beams. He then split logs into long planks for siding and cut small square shingles for the roof. Once the barn was built, mud and straw were stuffed into any cracks between the siding to keep out the wind.

Bank barn

Bank barns were built into the side of a small hill, or **bank**, which is how they got their name. The bank helped keep the barn cool in summer and warm in winter, and it also served as a ramp to the barn's upper floor. Straw and hay were stored on this level. To spare himself the tiring work of lifting and pitching straw and hay, a farmer simply drove his loaded wagon up the ramp to the second floor and unloaded it. Animals were kept in stalls and pens on the ground floor of the barn.

There were two types of bank barns—the Pennsylvania and the Sweitzer. Both had stone foundations, but the upper stories of Sweitzer barns were made of wood, and Pennsylvania barns were built entirely of stone or brick. The wooden siding of the bank barn above was replaced with aluminum.

Round and octagonal barns

Most early settlers had strong religious beliefs. One religious group, called the Shakers, wanted to show that it was different from other groups. Shakers chose the circle to be their symbol because they believed that it was the most perfect shape created by God. They wore circular hats, wove circular rugs, and many built circular barns. The round barns required less wood or stone to build than square or rectangular barns and housed more hay and animals. Best of all, round barns had no corners in which the devil could hide!

Connected barns

Most connected barns were made up of several small buildings, arranged in an L or U shape, and joined by one roof. A connected barn often surrounded the barnyard, sheltering it from driving winds and snow. Some farmers connected the barn to their house so they would not have to go outside to do their chores during the cold winter.

Sod barns

When pioneers moved west, they could not build wooden barns because there were not enough trees on the prairie. There were vast areas of grass, however, so the western settlers built sod barns. To make walls, the pioneers cut blocks of sod from the ground and stacked them like bricks. For the roof, they laid strips of sod over a frame that they had made with poles.

In the winter, the farmer at this house can tend to the livestock in his small connected barn without going outside.

Note: Although women also worked on the farm, a man was considered the head of the family and was called the farmer.

Pioneers on the prairies used a sod barn until they could afford to build one of brick, stone, or wood, which were shipped from elsewhere.

Inside the barn

Most barns had two floors. The animals lived on the first floor. Wagons, tools, and other equipment were also stored there. Farmers kept straw and hay on the second floor.

In early barns, such as this one, grains were stored in a bin on the **threshing floor**. Later, when harvests and barns became larger, an entire room, called a **granary**, was used to store grains.

Wide double doors led to the threshing floor, where many chores were done. Sheaves of grain were spread on the floor to be threshed. The sheaves were hit over and over again to separate the grains from their stalks. Other jobs, such as winnowing, repairing tools, and sheep shearing, were done on the threshing floor as well. Work parties were also held in this area of the barn.

Farmers dropped hay or straw onto the threshing floor through an opening called a **hay bay**.

Hay, fed to animals during winter, and straw, used as bedding, were stored in the **hayloft** or **mow**.

Equipment was also stored in the barn when it was not needed.

This trap door led to a manure cellar below the barn. Dirty straw and manure were pushed down the hole.

11

A barn-raising bee

Most pioneer families built their first small barn by themselves, but when they needed a larger barn, their neighbors gathered for a barn-raising **bee**. A bee combined a difficult job with a party. At a barn-raising bee, neighbors brought their tools and worked together to raise and secure the frame for a new barn.

Preparing for the bee

The farmer began working on the barn more than a year before the day of the bee. He spent months chopping down trees, removing their bark, and cutting them into square beams. The beams were left to **season**, or dry, for a year. It was important for the wood to season, or it would shrink later and cause the barn to leak. When the wood was ready, the farmer used a team of oxen or horses to haul the beams to the building site. He then constructed the **bents**, or sections of the barn's frame, on the ground. The frames of most barns were made up of four or five bents.

The big day

On the day of the bee, workers raised the bents using ropes and long poles with metal spikes on their ends. It took many strong arms to set the heavy bents in place! Some workers had the dangerous job of climbing up the frame to join the bents. After the frame was secured, workers attached **rafters** to the top of the bents. Rafters were the beams that supported the roof, which the farmer added later.

Raising the barn's frame was a difficult and dangerous job. The workers were proud of their hard work, and many carved their name or initials, along with the date of the barn raising, into one of the beams. A roof tree was attached to the rafters for good luck. After the frame was up, everyone enjoyed a huge dinner that the women had spent days preparing. Singing, dancing, and games continued into the night.

Holding the barn together

The beams in a barn were not hammered together with metal nails. When the bents were properly positioned, workers connected them by sliding a square bar, called a **tenon**, on one beam into the hole, called a **mortise**, of another. A wooden peg, or **trunnel**, was then pounded into the joint to hold the beams together. These joints were very secure—many barns that were built a hundred years ago are still standing today!

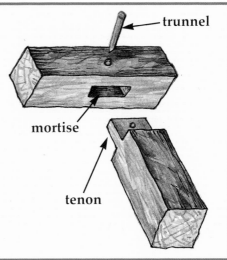

trunnel

mortise

tenon

Barn tools and gadgets

Most tools found in and around early barns were made by the farmers. Metal was scarce and expensive, so the tools were made of wood. Later, metals such as iron became more common, and tools were usually forged by a local blacksmith.

*A farmer used a **flail** to thresh grains. A flail was a long wooden handle attached to a thick pole by a leather strap. The farmer held the handle and swung the pole down onto the sheaves again and again to knock the grains off their stalks.*

*A **winnowing tray** was used to separate grains from their husks, or **chaff**. Grain was put in the tray and then tossed into the air. The light chaff was blown away by the wind, and the heavy grain fell to the floor.*

Fire safety was always a concern. A tin lantern, which held a candle, protected dry straw from the candle flame.

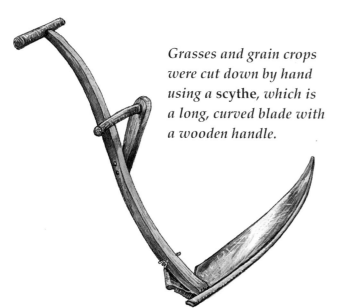

*Grasses and grain crops were cut down by hand using a **scythe**, which is a long, curved blade with a wooden handle.*

*Piled-up hay settled and became tightly packed over time. Farmers had to use a **hay knife** to cut out chunks of hay.*

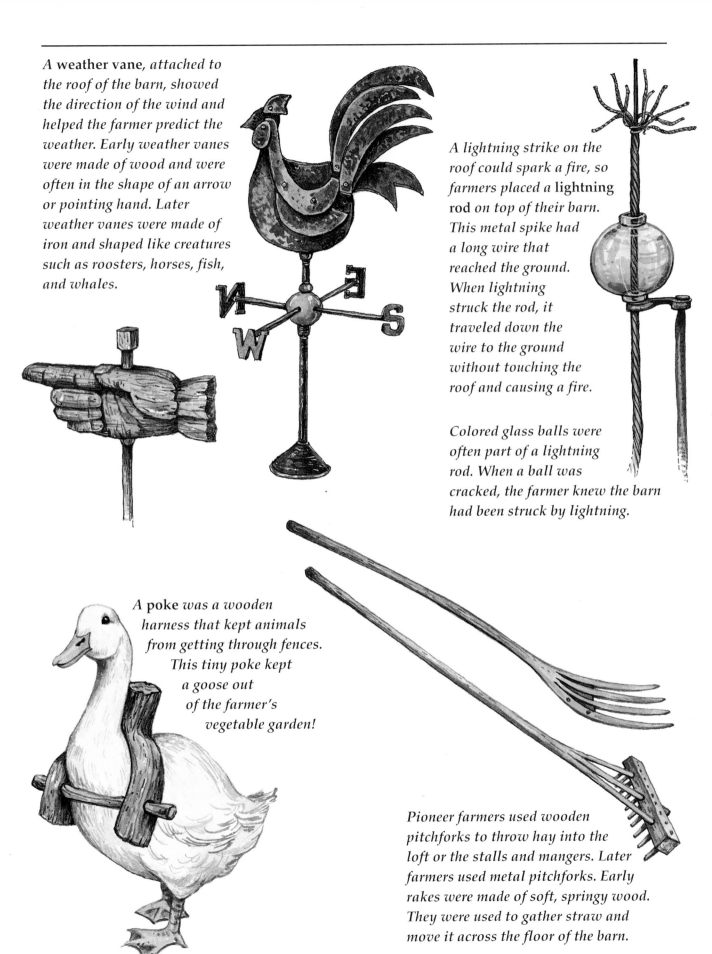

A **weather vane**, *attached to the roof of the barn, showed the direction of the wind and helped the farmer predict the weather. Early weather vanes were made of wood and were often in the shape of an arrow or pointing hand. Later weather vanes were made of iron and shaped like creatures such as roosters, horses, fish, and whales.*

A lightning strike on the roof could spark a fire, so farmers placed a **lightning rod** *on top of their barn. This metal spike had a long wire that reached the ground. When lightning struck the rod, it traveled down the wire to the ground without touching the roof and causing a fire.*

Colored glass balls were often part of a lightning rod. When a ball was cracked, the farmer knew the barn had been struck by lightning.

A **poke** *was a wooden harness that kept animals from getting through fences. This tiny poke kept a goose out of the farmer's vegetable garden!*

Pioneer farmers used wooden pitchforks to throw hay into the loft or the stalls and mangers. Later farmers used metal pitchforks. Early rakes were made of soft, springy wood. They were used to gather straw and move it across the floor of the barn.

Around the barnyard

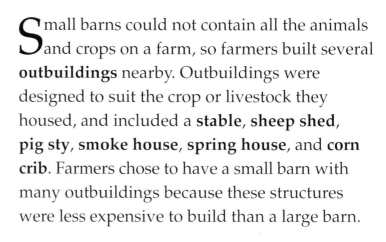

Small barns could not contain all the animals and crops on a farm, so farmers built several **outbuildings** nearby. Outbuildings were designed to suit the crop or livestock they housed, and included a **stable**, **sheep shed**, **pig sty**, **smoke house**, **spring house**, and **corn crib**. Farmers chose to have a small barn with many outbuildings because these structures were less expensive to build than a large barn.

① Sheep stayed out of the hot sun in a sheep shed, a building that had a roof but no walls.

② Horses and cows lived in a stable.

③ Corn on the cob is moist and can go moldy, so farmers stored it in a corn crib. Spaces in the walls allowed air to flow through the crib and keep the corn dry. The building was raised on posts, and a tin pan was nailed to the top of each post to keep mice from getting into the crib.

④ Pioneer farms did not have refrigerators or freezers in which to store meats. Farmers preserved, or cured, their meat in a smoke house. A small fire of bark or corn husks burned on the floor, and meat was hung on hooks above it. The smoke from the fire flavored the meat and preserved it.

⑤ Duck houses were built beside a pond. Some had a ramp that went from the house to the water.

⑥ Chickens lived in coops. Although glass windows were expensive, some farmers put them in their chicken coops. They found that chickens laid more eggs when they had lots of sunlight.

⑦ Most early farms were located near springs so there was a constant supply of water for the farm. A spring is an opening in the ground, out of which water flows. A small spring house was built over a cold-water spring. The family placed jugs and crocks of milk, butter, and cheese in the cold water to keep the foods from spoiling. The house protected the food from hungry animals and also kept the water clean.

⑧ Pigs lived in a sty. Many pig sties had a swinging door that opened into the yard or a fenced pig run.

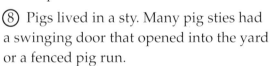

Barnyard animals

Livestock was necessary on the early farms. Large, strong animals helped with heavy work such as plowing and pulling wagons and sleds. Farmers also kept a variety of animals to provide the family with leather, wool, food, and fat for cooking and making candles and soap.

Milk
Families kept cows to supply them with milk, cheese, and butter. Some could not afford a cow, so they kept goats instead. Cows and goats were fed grass and clover to make their milk sweet. They were milked every morning and evening.

Work animals

Most farmers had a team of oxen or work horses. Oxen are large male cattle. They were especially important on early farms because they were strong enough to pull out tree stumps and clear heavy boulders from the land. Once the land was cleared, many farmers kept work horses. They were not as strong as oxen, but they moved much faster. Work animals also pulled the plow, wagon, and sled on the settler farm. Later, they pulled heavy machinery such as mowers and combines.

Pigs ate the leftovers from the family's kitchen. When they got fat, they were butchered and cut into chops, sausages, and bacon. Their fat was used for cooking and making candles and soap.

Many farmers kept a dog or two to help them herd animals in the field and bring them to the barn. At night, the dog patrolled the barnyard, protecting the livestock from hungry wild animals.

Sheep were useful to the family because of their fleece, which was cut, cleaned, combed, and spun into yarn. The yarn was woven into warm wool fabric that was used to make clothing and blankets. Sheep also provided the family with another source of meat.

Poultry

Most farmers raised at least one type of **poultry**. Poultry includes birds such as chickens, turkeys, ducks, and geese. All these birds were a source of meat and eggs. Their feathers were used to stuff pillows and quilts. If a farmer did not have a dog, geese were often the "guards" of the barnyard. They honked loudly to frighten away intruders or gave them a painful nip with their beaks.

Mousers

Cats were kept inside the barn to act as **mousers**. They killed mice and rats, which were a big problem in the granary. These pests ate and dirtied the grain that was stored for the family and livestock to eat. They also spread diseases such as **typhus**, which was carried by the ticks and fleas on their bodies.

Children's chores

There was so much work to do on a pioneer farm that everyone in the family had lots of chores. Most children began helping with farm work when they were five years old. Each child had a set of chores to do around the barnyard every morning and evening. In the spring and summer, when there was a lot of field work to do as well, children stayed home from school and worked all day on the farm. Some did not attend school at all and helped on the farm all year.

Feeding the animals

Each morning, the children fed the livestock. They emptied a pail of kitchen scraps into the pig trough and scattered corn for the barnyard birds. While the chickens were eating, one of the children went into the coop to collect their eggs.

During warm months, the children did not feed grazing animals such as sheep and cows. They sent them to eat grass in the pastures. In winter, these animals stayed in the barnyard, and the children fed them hay every day.

Mucking out the stalls

The animals' stalls and pens were cleaned, or **mucked out**, once a day. Manure and old straw were gathered and removed with a manure fork. Fresh straw was then spread in each pen and stall.

Grooming the horses

One of the older children cared for the horses. The horses' hooves and shoes had to be inspected every morning. A horse could be injured from walking all day on a loose shoe or a stone caught in its hoof.

At the end of the day, the horses' sweaty coats were wiped dry, and their tired muscles were massaged. Their coats were brushed, and the tangles were combed from their manes and tails.

Milking time

One of the children milked the cow twice a day. The child sat on a small stool and rested his or her forehead against the cow's side to keep the animal from moving. It took a lot of practice to milk a cow. If a milker pulled too hard, the cow would refuse to "let down" its milk!

A child carried water to the animals every morning. It took as many as thirty trips to the well to fill all the troughs! Buckets were carried on a yoke to make the job a little easier.

In the evening, one of the children went out to the pastures to herd the cows and sheep. He or she took them to the barn for the night, where they were safe from wild animals.

Through the seasons

Farmers and their families rarely enjoyed a break from working. Each season brought a different set of chores. Most people, however, welcomed the change in their daily routine.

Spring

In the spring, farmers spent most of their time plowing the fields, mending fences, and planting new crops, but there was still work to be done around the barn. Sleighs and sleds were pulled into the barn, where they were stored until winter. During rainy days, farmers repaired tools and split firewood inside the barn. Most farmers whitewashed or painted their barn each spring.

Spring was also a time when many farm animals gave birth. A farmer often had to help with the delivery of baby animals. If the mother died, her babies were cared for by the farmer's children.

In the spring, sheep were washed and their fleece removed with sharp shears. The fleece was cut off carefully in a single, thick sheet.

Many baby animals, including piglets, were born in the spring.

Summer

During the summer, most of the work took place in the fields. Crops had to be watered, weeded, and checked for bugs. Near the end of summer, the family worked together to cut down wheat and other grains and move them to the barn for storage. They also mowed meadows and stored the sweet grasses and clover to feed their animals over the winter. Much of this work, called **haying**, was done at night, when the air was cooler.

While parents worked in the fields, children played hide-and-seek among the haystacks.

Autumn

Fall was one of the busiest times around the barn. On windy days, the family threshed and winnowed all the grain they harvested and stored it in the granary. Animals that could not be fed over the winter were slaughtered. The butchered animals were hung in the smoke house or stored in barrels of salt water, or **brine**. Poultry was plucked, and the feathers were stuffed into comforters and mattresses. After preserving enough meat for its own use, the family took extra livestock to market. The family also gathered fruits and vegetables to dry or store in the cellar.

Apples were a useful crop. They were stored fresh in the cellar, cut into strips and dried, and made into applesauce, cider, and vinegar. Most families held work parties in their barn to get neighbors to help peel the many bushels of apples.

Winter

During the winter, the farmer spent much of his time working indoors. He brought plows, harrows, wagons, and carts into the barn, where he got them ready for work in the spring. He also repaired harnesses and tools and sharpened the blade of the plow.

The family finished threshing and winnowing any grain that had not been done in the fall. The farmer frequently visited the granary to make sure pests had not gotten into the grain bins.

The cows, horses, and sheep needed a lot of care in the winter. They could not go out to the snowy pastures to find food, so they had to be fed and given water every day. The farmer made sure that the animals were warm. He let fresh air into the barn so the animals would not get sick.

The farmer and his children spent much of their time each day tending to the animals in the barn.

Fun and frolic in the barn

Sometimes jobs such as corn husking, apple peeling, and threshing were too big for family members to finish on their own, so they held a work party, or **bee**, to get help from their neighbors. Bees were also called **frolics**. Neighbors were eager to help because they, too, would need help with work on their own farm. Since pioneer farms were far apart, people were not able to visit often with their neighbors. They welcomed the chance to tell jokes and stories while they worked.

Teams and contests

To make a big task more fun, people often made it into a contest. They worked in teams to peel apples and husk corn. Each team tried to finish their pile of corn or apples first.

At apple-peeling frolics, young people tried to peel the skin from their apple in one long strip. If they did, they threw the peel into the air, hoping that it would land in the shape of a letter. It was believed that the letter would be the first initial of their future husband or wife.

Full stomachs and happy feet

When the work was finished, everyone was invited to enjoy a huge potluck meal. A barn dance, complete with fiddlers and other musicians, ended the evening on a happy note.

Look for the young man who has found an ear of red corn. He has won a type of contest. Now he can kiss the young woman of his choice. Some men cheated at this game, however, and brought a cob of red corn in their pocket!

Do you know why?

Do you know why legend has it that cattle speak on Christmas Eve?
Farmers used to tell their children that the cattle spoke on Christmas Eve, and that it was bad luck for anyone to hear them. This superstition kept the children away from the barn while their parents were busy hiding small Christmas gifts inside. The belief came from the legend that, when Jesus was born, the animals in the stable spoke.

Do you know why some farmers painted special symbols on their barns?
Some people believed witches could cast **hexes**, or magic spells, to make animals sick, turn the hay moldy, or start a fire. Pennsylvania Dutch farmers painted these colorful designs, called **hex signs**, on their barns to protect them from bad luck or magic.

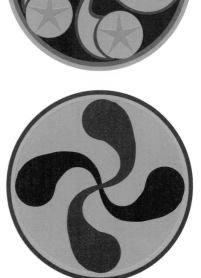

Glossary

cellar A cool place used for storage, located beneath a house or barn or dug into a hillside

chaff The husks of rye, oats, wheat, or other grains

combine A machine that harvests and threshes grain at the same time

forge To heat metal and then shape it using a hammer

foundation The base of a building

frame A structure that gives shape to and supports a building

granary A storage area for grain

harrow A heavy wooden farm tool with spikes on one side, used to break up soil

hay Various plants, such as clover, grass, and alfalfa, that are cut and dried for use as livestock feed

mow The space in a barn where hay or grain is stored

mower A machine for cutting down hay or grain

pasture A field or meadow where animals such as cows, sheep, horses, or other animals graze

Pennsylvania Dutch Describing people who are descended from the Swiss and Germans who settled in Pennsylvania in the 1600s and 1700s

poultry Domestic birds such as chickens, turkeys, geese, and ducks

prairie A vast, treeless area of grassland

Shakers A Christian religious group, originally from England, named for their custom of dancing with shaking movements during ceremonies

shear To clip the fleece off sheep

shears A large pair of sharp scissors

sheaves Bundles of hay or grain

siding Wood or other material covering the outside of a frame building

sod A grassy piece cut from the ground, usually in a square or strip

straw The dry stalks or stems of various grains, such as wheat, oats, barley, or rye

thresh To separate grain from chaff, usually with a flail or threshing machine

typhus Any of a group of diseases, carried and spread by lice and fleas, that cause headaches, high fevers, and spotted rashes

whitewash A white-colored mixture of lime and water used to paint walls and fences

winnow To separate grain from chaff

yoke A wooden bar worn across the neck and shoulders, used for carrying or pulling heavy loads

Index

Acknowledgments

Photographs and reproductions

Gift of Maxim Karolik to the Karolik Collection of American Paintings, 1815-1865; Courtesy, Museum of Fine Arts, Boston: pages 28-29
Black Creek Pioneer Village, Metro Toronto and Region Conservation Authority: page 5 (bottom)
Bronte Provincial Park: page 24 (bottom)
Marc Crabtree, at Genesee Country Museum: pages 22 (both), 23 (both)
Alex Demyan: page 18
Terry Donnelly/Tom Stack & Associates: pages 7, 8
Georgia Agrirama: page 19 (bottom)

Bobbie Kalman: pages 9 (top, at Black Creek Pioneer Village), 21
Living History Farms, Iowa: title page, pages 20 (both), 24 (top)
Bob Mansur: pages 5 (top), 6 (top)
National Museum of American Art, Washington DC/Art Resource, NY: pages 25, 27
New York State Historical Association, Cooperstown: page 26
Joseph Stanski/Morning Star Photo: page 19 (top)

Illustrations and colorizations

Barbara Bedell: cover, pages 3, 4, 6, 9, 10-11, 12-13, 14-15, 16-17, 25, 27

3 4 5 6 7 8 9 0   Printed in the U.S.A.   6 5 4 3 2 1 0 9